A. DANNHÄUSER

Solfège des Solfèges

Translated by

J. H. CORNELL

IN THREE BOOKS

G. SCHIRMER, Inc.

DISTRIBUTED BY

HAL•LEONARD®
CORPORATION

7777 W. BLUEMOUND RD. P.O. BOX 13819 MILWAUKEE, WI 53213

Preparatory Exercises.
For the Intonations.

These exercises are made in order to familiarise the pupil with the intonations, and for sparing him the necessity of solving two difficulties at a time; the duration of the values and the accuracy of the sounds; hence, he will have to practise them exclusively while he is learning the first chapters of principles.

When the pupil shall seize the intonations easily, he will have to practise in beating two, three and four to the measure, counting the beats instead of naming the notes, or of solfeggiating them. For this exercise, he should observe the greatest equality in the duration of each beat. (1)

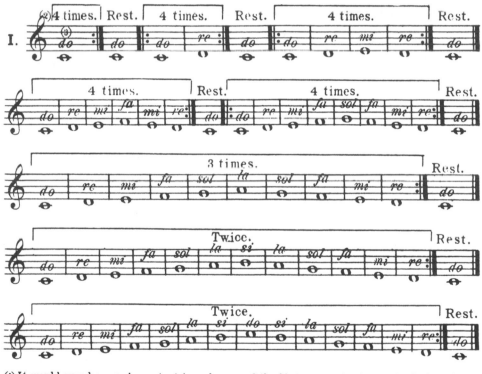

(1) It would even be very important to make use of the Metronome for this work, which ought to be done at different degrees of slowness and of quickness.

The first labor, made with care, will give great ease to all that shall follow; it belongs, however, to teachers or to mothers of families beginning with young children in this so essential part of the art, to guide them, according to their youthful intelligence.

(2) Each exercise should be made as many times as indicated. It would be well that the teacher should execute it alone the first time, letting the pupil repeat it immediately.

(3) Let the pupil hold each note as long as his breath will allow him, without fatigue, and let him rest for a measure, in silence, at all the rests indicated.

9593 r   *Copyright, 1891, by G. Schirmer*   Printed in the U.S.A.

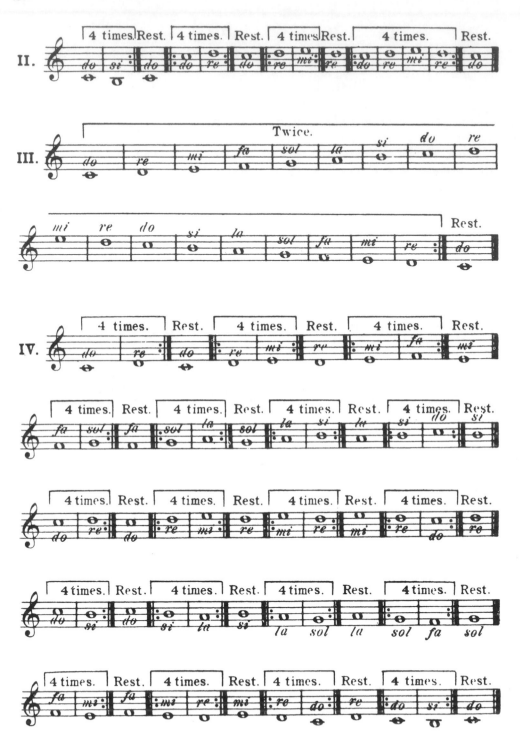

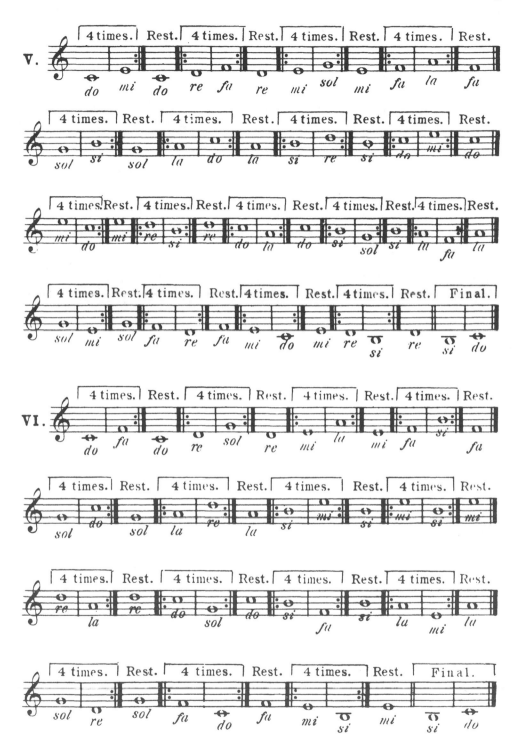

Scale of the tone C *(do)*, major mode.

Four beats to the measure.

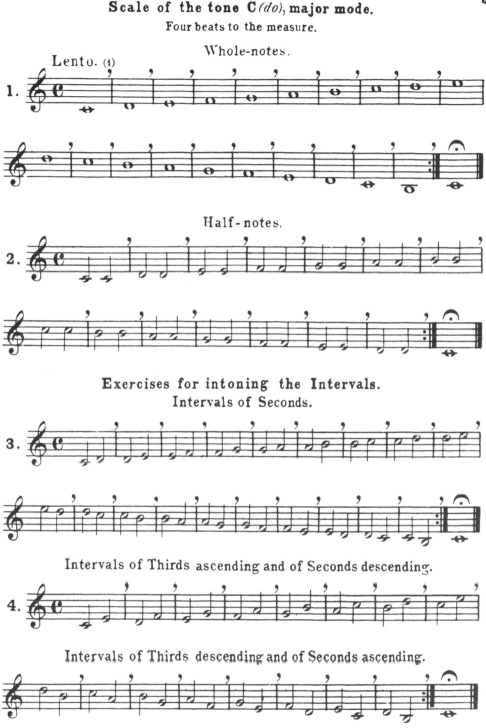

Whole-notes.

Lento. (1)

Half-notes.

Exercises for intoning the Intervals.
Intervals of Seconds.

Intervals of Thirds ascending and of Seconds descending.

Intervals of Thirds descending and of Seconds ascending.

6

Intervals of Fourths ascending and of Thirds descending.

5.

Intervals of Fourths descending and of Thirds ascending.

Intervals of Fifths ascending and of Fourths descending.

6.

Intervals of Fifths descending and of Fourths ascending.

Intervals of Sixths ascending and of Fifths descending.

7.

Intervals of Sixths descending and of Fifths ascending.

Intervals of Sevenths ascending and of Sixths descending.

Intervals of Sevenths descending and of Sixths ascending.

8.

Intervals of Octaves ascending and of Sevenths descending.

Intervals of Octaves descending and of Sevenths ascending.

9.

Summary of the Intervals.

Lessons
for the different note-values and the different kinds of measure.
Lessons with Whole-notes and Whole-note rests.
The rest is the silence of the Whole-note.
Moderato.*) The Whole-note counts four beats.

Lessons with Half-notes and Half-note rests.
The half-note rest is the silence of the half-note.
The Half-note counts two beats.

*) For all the elementary lessons, the movement "*Moderato*" with 4 beats ought always to be metronomed 100 or 104 for each beat, or quarter-note.

Lessons with Whole-notes and Half-notes.

Lessons with Quarter- notes and their rests.
The Quarter-note rest is the silence of the Quarter-note.
The Quarter-note counts one beat.

Lesson with Quarter-notes and one Quarter-note rest at the **first** beat.

Lesson with Quarter-notes and one Quarter-note rest at the **second** beat.

Lesson with Quarter-notes and one Quarter-note rest at the **third** beat.

Lesson with Quarter-notes and one Quarter-note rest at the **fourth** beat.

Lesson with Quarter-notes and one Quarter-note
rest at the second and the fourth beat.

Lessons with Half-notes and Quarter-notes.

Lessons with Whole-notes, Half-notes and Quarter-notes.

Lessons with Eighth-notes and Eighth-note rests.

The Eighth-note rest is the silence of the Eighth-note.
Two Eighth-notes to a beat, or one Eighth-note and its rest.

14

Andante. ($\bullet$ = 80) ROD.

39.

Lesson with Half-notes and Eighth-notes.

Andante. ($\bullet$ = 76) ROD.

40.

Lesson with Quarter-notes and Eighth-notes.

Moderato assai. ($\bullet$ = 80) H.L.

41.

Fine.

Lesson with Half-notes, Quarter-notes, and Eighth-notes.

Lesson with Whole-notes, Half-notes, Quarter-notes and Eighth-notes.

Lessons for 3/4 measure.
One dotted Half-note to the measure, one Quarter-note to each beat.
The dotted Half note counts three beats.

Fine.

The Half-note counts two beats and the Quarter-note one beat.

Two Eighth- notes to one beat.

Andante. (♩ = 84)   G.C.

49.

Lessons for the 2/2 measure, or C
One Whole-note to the measure.

Allegro. (♩ = 96)   ROD.

50.

18

One Half-note to a beat.

9593

The preceding lesson reduced to Quarter-notes.

Lessons for ²⁄4 measure.

A Half-note to the whole measure, a Quarter-note to a beat.

Allegretto. ($\bullet$ = 92)

H.L.

A Quarter-note or two Eighth-notes to the beat.

Andantino. ($\bullet$ = 70)

H.L.

N⁰ 31 reduced to Eighth-notes.

Moderato. ($\bullet$ = 80)

ROD.

Lessons for the use of dotted notes in C and ₵ measures.
The dotted Half-note counts three beats in ⁴⁄4 measure.

Andantino. ($\bullet$ = 88)

G.C.

The dotted Half-note counts a beat and a half in **C** measure.

Moderato.(♩ = 80)

ROD.

63.

Fine.

Reduction of the preceding Lesson.

A dotted Quarter-note counts three quarters of a beat in 2/2 (**C**) measure.

Andante.(♩ = 60)

ROD.

64.

Fine.

A dotted Quarter-note counts one beat and a half in 4/4(**C**) measure.

Moderato. (♩ = 72)

G. C.

65.

9593

Moderato.($\downarrow$ = 80)

ROD.

66.

Fine.

Lesson with Sixteenths.

Andante.($\downarrow$ = 63) Four sixteenths for one beat.

H. L.

67.

Fine.

One Quarter - note, or two Eighth - notes, or four Sixteenth notes
Andante assai.($\downarrow$ = 112)   to a beat.

68.

Moderato. ($\quad$=76) Reduction of lesson 66.

ROD.

69.

Fine.

Andante. ($\quad$=120)

G. C.

70.

Lessons for ⅜ measure.
One Eighth-note to one beat, one Quarter-note to two beats,
the dotted Quarter-note to the whole measure.

Andantino. ($\quad$=100)

II. L.

71.

Fine.

Two sixteenths to one beat.

Andante assai.($\bullet$ = 100)

G.C.

Lessons for 6/8 measure.
A dotted Quarter-note, or three Eighth-notes, to one beat.

Andantino.($\bullet$ = 54)

H.L.

Fine.

Moderato.($\bullet$ = 60)

H.L.

Fine.

A Quarter-note and an Eighth-note to a beat.

Lessons with Triplets.

Lesson for the regular Syncope with Half-notes.

Allegro. (♩ = 92)

G. C.

Lesson for the regular Syncope with Quarter-notes.

Moderato. (♩ = 96)

G. C.

Lesson for the regular Syncope with Eighth-notes.

Exercise for the study of the first sharp on Fa.

Moderato.($\downarrow$ = 96)

H.L.

84.

Fine.

Exercise for the study of Fa sharp and Do sharp.

Andantino.($\downarrow$ = 80)

H.L.

85.

Exercise for the study of three sharps: Fa, Do and Sol.

Moderato.(♩= 80)

H.L.

86.

Exercise for the study of four sharps: Fa, Do, Sol and Re.

Andante.(♩= 72)

H. L.

87.

Exercise for the study of five sharps: Fa, Do, Sol, Re and La.

Moderato.(♩= 88)

H.L.

88.

Lesson in major mode of Do, with the use of the first five accidental sharps.

Moderato. (♩ = 92)   G.C.

93.

Exercise for intoning Si flat.

Exercise for intoning Si flat and Mi flat.

Exercise for intoning the three flats; Si, Mi and La.

Exercise for intoning the four flats; Si, Mi, La and Re.

Lesson in the major mode of Do, with the first four accidental flats.

Chromatic Scale in Do, major mode.

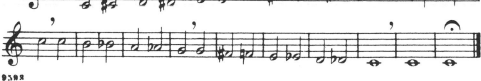

Scale of the tone La, minor mode.
Parallel of the scale of Do, major mode.

Lessons in the minor mode of La.

Reduction of the 103d lesson.

Moderato (♩= 104)

H.L.

109.

Fine. *f*

poco a poco cresc.

Allegro. (♩= 132)

R.O.D.

110.

un poco cresc.

Allegro moderato.(♩ = 120)

R O D.

Scale of the tone Mi, minor mode.
Parallel of Sol, major mode.

Lento.(♩ = 60)

Lessons in the minor mode of Mi.

Moderato.(♩ = 104)

H. L.

Allegro. ($\downarrow$ = 72)

HASSE.

117.

Scale of the tone Fa, major mode.

Lento ($\downarrow$ = 60)

118.

Lessons in the major mode of Fa.

Moderato. ($\downarrow$ = 100)

H. L.

119.

Fine.

44

Scale of the tone Re, minor mode.
Parallel of Fa, major mode.

Lessons in the minor mode of Re.

9593

Moderato.(♩=84) ROD.

127.

Affettuoso. (♩.=72) HASSE.

128.

Scale of the tone Re, major mode.

Lessons in the major mode of Re.

9393

Moderato (♩ = 100) H. L.

132.

Fine.

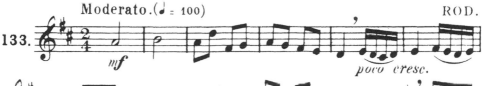

Moderato. (♩ = 100) ROD.

133.

48

Scale of the tone Si, minor mode.
Parallel of Re, major mode.

Lessons in the minor mode of Si.

9593

Scale of the tone Si♭, major mode.

137. Lento (♩= 60)

Lessons in the major mode of Si♭.

138. Moderato (♩= 132)   ROD.

139. Andantino. (♩= 63)   H.L.

9593

Of the Fa-Clef (Bass-Clef.)

Example of the compass of the (Fa-Clef) for the Piano.

Notes in the Sol-clef corresponding to those in the Fa.

Exercise in the compass of the Soprano Voice. *)

Cause the notes to be named.and let them afterwards be solfeggiated if it be thought necessary; in which case let the time be counted by beating two to the measure.

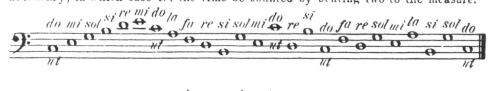

Allegretto. (♩ = 100)

H.L.

147.

*) Soprano or Contralto voices (women or children) executing music written in the Fa-clef, will sound it an Octave above the notation.

Moderato. (♩ = 96)   G.C.

156.

Moderato. (♩ = 60)   H.L.

157.

a tempo.

Waltz movement. (♪ = 152)

H.L.

161.

Andante ma non troppo. (♩.= 60)

H.L.

162.

Allegretto (♩ = 108)

H.L.

163.

Moderato. (♩ = 112)

H.L.

164.

Allegret. ($\flat$ = 138)   H.L.

165.

9593

Moderato. (♩ = 112)

ROD.

166.

Doloroso. (♩ = 72)

H. L.

167.

dolce ed espress.

dolce

p

dolce

dolce

morendo

Allegro (♩.= 96)

ROD.

168.

Allegro moderato. (♩ = 96)

ROD.

171.